DONATELLO

AT CLOSE RANGE

D1540934

Frontispiece. Detail of *St John on Patmos*. After cleaning, in raking light.

DONATELLO
AT CLOSE RANGE

An initial view of
THE RESTORATION OF THE STUCCOES
in the
OLD SACRISTY, S. LORENZO, FLORENCE

by

Fabrizio Bandini, Guido Botticelli, Cristina Danti,
Isabella Lapi Ballerini, Mauro Matteini and Arcangelo Moles,
of the Opificio delle Pietre Dure, Florence
and Maurizio Seracini, E. di Tech., Florence

with introduction by

Caroline Elam

PHOTOGRAPHIC DOCUMENTATION SPONSORED BY THE

SAMUEL H. KRESS FOUNDATION

WORLD MONUMENTS FUND

SAMUEL H. KRESS FOUNDATION

THE BURLINGTON MAGAZINE

———— 1987 ————

The essays in this catalogue are translated versions of the contributions to
Donatello e la Sagrestia Vecchia di San Lorenzo: Temi, studi, proposte di un cantiere di restauro, catalogue published by Centro Di, Florence, 1986.

The original exhibition in S. Lorenzo, Florence (20th June-13th September 1986) was organised by Cristina Danti and Isabella Lapi Ballerini of the Opificio delle Pietre Dure e Laboratori di Restauro di Firenze, and Pietro Ruschi and Carlo Sisi of the Soprintendenza per i Beni Ambientali e Architettonici per le provincie di Firenze e Pistoia, under the auspices of the Ministero per i Beni Culturali e Ambientali and the Comune di Firenze.

The exhibition was designed by Pietro Ruschi, with the collaboration of Raoul Paggetta.

Photographs by: Gabinetto Fotografico della Soprintendenza per i Beni Ambientali e Architettonici di Firenze e Pistoia, Gabinetto Fotografico dell'Opificio delle Pietre Dure e Laboratori di Restauro, Paolo Brandinelli, Conway Library (Courtauld Institute of Art). The black and white photographs in raking light are by E. di Tech., s.r.l.

The English version of the catalogue was first published in the March 1987 issue of the Burlington magazine

© The Burlington Magazine Publications Limited, 1987

ISBN 0 9511350 1 5

Catalogue designed by Kevin Shenton

Typeset in Monotype Lasercomp Van Dijck
Printed by Jolly & Barber Ltd, Rugby, Warwickshire

Foreword

The 600th anniversary of Donatello's birth in 1386 provided the occasion for a number of celebrations during the past year, most notably, of course, in Florence. One especially imaginative and unrepeatable event took place in the Old Sacristy of the church of San Lorenzo, where the Opificio delle Pietre Dure and the Soprintendenza dei Beni Ambientali e Architettonici invited the public to view at first hand the completed first stage of their joint restoration featuring the newly restored stucco reliefs by Donatello on the altar wall. It was a stunning revelation.

Normally inaccessible at the top of the Sacristy, and previously dulled by grime, Donatello's three roundels of St John the Evangelist – a portrait of a saint in meditation, a lyrical landscape portraying his vision at Patmos, and a more violent scene of his martyrdom – could be seen in the freshness and immediacy of the artist's eye-view by anyone who climbed to the top of the carpeted scaffold. Pairs of standing saints by Donatello and his collaborators and a cheerful frieze of angelic heads in the manner of Luca della Robbia were likewise newly visible as fully half of the Sacristy recovered long-lost beauty. By sharing their discoveries before commencing the remainder of the restoration campaign, the authorities made a major contribution to the Donatello year. In a nearby room off the cloister, a handsome didactic exhibition with full-scale colour reproductions and comparative views of work in progress offered further information to the interested visitor. An exemplary catalogue★ explains this technical data in detail.

Both the exhibition and the catalogue utilised materials made possible by a grant from the Samuel H. Kress Foundation to the World Monuments Fund. The contribution enabled the scientific group E.Di.Tech. of Florence to conduct more sophisticated analyses and more extensive photography during the course of the restoration than was permitted by the restricted Italian budgets for the project. The scientific data contributed to the interpretations put forward in the Florentine catalogue, in part translated here for an English audience. The primary purpose of the present publication is, however, to offer an initial view of the restored stuccoes and the vivid proximity to Donatello captured by the raking-light photography.

In themselves, the extraordinary beauty of the works of art, and the supreme importance of the artist, warranted the participation of the Kress Foundation. Moreover, the project exemplifies a cherished tenet of the Foundation's philosophy, that a limited but timely contribution to meet a well-defined need may reap significant results. In this instance, two major programme areas – concern for the preservation of important artistic monuments, and the promotion of scholarly resources in the history of art – have been jointly served. So well, indeed, that the Kress Foundation has joined the World Monuments Fund in sponsoring an international tour for the original Florentine exhibition.

To the extent that reproduction allows, both the exhibition and the publication of this material are a means of sharing these genuinely 'rediscovered' works by Donatello with a larger audience. The outstanding quality of the photography by Maurizio Seracini brings us close to the intimate view of the Old Sacristy which, for a brief moment in the summer of 1986, a fortunate few were privileged to enjoy.

MARILYN PERRY
President
Samuel H. Kress Foundation

★*Donatello e la Sagrestia Vecchia di San Lorenzo. Temi, studi, proposte di un cantiere di restauro* (Centro Di, Florence, 1986).

1. Detail from *St John Evangelist*. After cleaning, in raking light.

Preface

For nearly twenty years the World Monuments Fund★ has been supporting the restoration of Italian artistic treasures. In this period of time, the imperative for conservation of important works of art and historic buildings has risen into an international ground swell. As the techniques for evaluating and treating conservation problems have become more sophisticated, the urgency for broader exchange of scientific knowledge, for experienced professionals and for increased funding to support all these activities has also become more acute.

The World Monuments Fund is the only private non-profit organisation dedicated to alleviating this intense shortage by sponsoring preservation activity on an international basis. Recognising the inability of governments to budget adequately for cultural preservation, WMF seeks to complement government funding, to respond to emergency situations, and to work with local preservation groups to multiply their capabilities. Training of professionals and the sponsorship of scientific study are important components of the organisation's programme, since both training and research are integral parts of the preservation process. Our highest mandate, however, is not to restore works which will inevitably need treatment again in the future, but to educate the public concerning the need for ongoing care, repair, and study of our great monuments. Perhaps the most important long-term effect we can have is to instil in the general public an appreciation of what restoration can accomplish, and how it affects our understanding of art and history.

The conservation now underway of the Donatello stuccoes in the Old Sacristy of San Lorenzo is one of the many dramatic examples, in this context, of rediscoveries being made in Italy through conservation. Thanks to generous support from the Samuel H. Kress Foundation, the World Monuments Fund has been able to participate in this discovery process, by supporting analytical photographic studies of the stuccoes under restoration, and sponsoring both an international travelling exhibition of these photographs and their publication in these pages, together with detailed conservation reports on the project.

We believe this material will be of interest on many levels. It chronicles a well structured conservation campaign and records the discoveries that were made in the course of it; it provides scholars and connoisseurs with a rare opportunity to view such works from the intimate perspective of the conservator. And for the general public, it provides a first opportunity to enjoy these little-known jewels. The restoration of the stuccoes not only improves their current state of health and contributes to their future security; it also returns to the public a group of major works that were, for practical purposes, lost. Lost, in obscurity, on the very walls of one of the greatest renaissance edifices in the heart of Florence! This is, indeed, why preservation is important.

BONNIE BURNHAM
Executive Director
World Monuments Fund

★Chartered in 1965 in New York under the name International Fund for Monuments.

2. The altar wall, Old Sacristy, S. Lorenzo, Florence.

Brunelleschi and Donatello in the Old Sacristy

CAROLINE ELAM

The Old Sacristy of S. Lorenzo is one of the first buildings of the Florentine renaissance and the only structure designed by the great architect Filippo Brunelleschi (1377-1446) that he saw completed during his lifetime. As an architectural and sculptural ensemble it inspired imitators all over Europe.

The Sacristy was commissioned by Giovanni di Bicci de'Medici (1360-1429), founder of the fortunes of the pre-eminent Florentine banking family, as part of the reconstruction of the church of S. Lorenzo. It was dedicated to Giovanni's patron saint, St John Evangelist – hence the subjects of Donatello's pendentive stuccoes – and was to function both as a sacristy, for storage and preparation of liturgical vestments and objects, and as a burial chapel for Giovanni and his descendants, where perpetual masses would be said by the special canons supported by the founder's endowment.

In an excellent study of the building's chronology, Pietro Ruschi has shown from new documents that the Old Sacristy was begun in 1422.[1] The date of its completion, 1428, was found inscribed on the lantern of the dome during the restoration of 1943. Giovanni di Bicci died the following year and was buried in a tomb designed by Brunelleschi's adopted son, Buggiano, in the centre of the Sacristy, below the dome. Pietro Ruschi has pointed out that the porphyry disk in the centre of the table over the tomb is exactly the same diameter as the base of the lantern, thus reinforcing the perfect geometries of Brunelleschi's building, and the symbolic relation of tomb (burial) and dome (resurrection), intended to recall the Holy Sepulchre in Jerusalem.

It was Giovanni's son, Cosimo il Vecchio (1389-1464), the leading political figure in Florence after 1434, who commissioned Donatello to complete the Sacristy's decoration. Donatello was the favourite sculptor of the Medici, and was to make for the family palace the bronze statues of David and Judith, as well as the bronze pulpits for S.Lorenzo itself. His works in the Sacristy are not recorded in any contemporary documents, and their dates have therefore been a matter for discussion. We know that Donatello was away in Rome from 1431-33, and that he left Florence for a ten-year stay in Padua in 1443.

A brief description of the structure of the Sacristy may be helpful for understanding the placing of Donatello's stucco reliefs and the problems their location caused him. The Old Sacristy is a simple square building, with a smaller square altar-chapel and two flanking rooms known as 'lavamani' (for ritual handwashing, storage, and access to crypt and roof). The altar wall (Fig.2) is articulated with grey stone pilasters which visually support the semi-circular mouldings of the lunette zone above. The ribbed 'umbrella' dome rests on four pendentives, triangular segments of masonry forming a concave curve, which serve to convert the square plan of the Sacristy into the circular ring at the base of the dome.

Donatello's interventions in the Old Sacristy were in two main areas: the tondi (roundels) of the pendentive and lunette

3. Section of the Old Sacristy, with elevation of the altar wall, showing the positions of Donatello's interventions.

zone, left blank by Brunelleschi, and the walls on either side of the altar chapel, where the the form of the doors had not yet been decided. Donatello filled the lunette roundels with stucco figures of the four evangelists (Fig.3; No.1), and those in the pendentives with scenes from the life of St John: his vision on Patmos (No.2), his attempted martyrdom in boiling oil (No.3), his raising of Drusiana, and his ascension. In the areas of wall between the pilasters on either side of the altar chapel, Donatello designed the door surrounds (No.4), and over these made stucco figures of the deacon saints, Stephen and Lawrence (No.5), and the Medici saints, Cosmas and Damian (No.6); later he modelled and cast the two pairs of bronze doors. Brunelleschi's biographer Antonio Manetti, writing in the 1480s, tells us that 'nothing in those small façades where the little doors are, between pilaster and pilaster, from the altar chapel to the side walls' is attributable to Brunelleschi, and that all this was the responsibility of Donatello, 'who did not understand much of the architectural side of sculpture'.[2] A heated exchange of sonnets took place between the two former friends, who had visited Rome and studied the ancient monuments together. Though we may disagree with Manetti's judgment of Donatello's unorthodox but inventive architectural detail, it is easy to see why Brunelleschi disliked these 'little facades': with their busy relief and strong projections, they filled up and cluttered his carefully balanced wall planes, blurring the distinction between architectural membering and wall, between grey stone and white plaster, that was so fundamental to his architectural aesthetic.

During the current conservation campaign, which is the subject of this catalogue, all the stuccoes of the altar wall have been analysed and cleaned, along with the astrological dome of the altar chapel and the other decorative details. Work will now begin on the remainder of the pendentive and lunette stuccoes. The cleaning, as well as revealing a series of superb works of art essentially for the first time, has provided extremely important technical evidence both for Donatello's working methods and the relationship of his sculptural interventions to the architecture that contains them. Undoubtedly the most thrilling discovery is that, as Cristina Danti explains below, Donatello made the stuccoes *in situ*, working very fast, modelling with his hands and a few, very simple tools. This is evident from the close-up photographs, too, which show eyes gouged with a stick or finger, tree-trunks formed of stucco strips like ribbons of pasta. The expressive power of the works to a modern eye derives partly from this evidence of speedy execution. Donatello was criticised in the fifteenth and sixteenth centuries for that neglect of 'finish' which to us makes his works both more moving and more accessible. He is not an artist who can be judged solely by the criteria of his period.

Art historians will continue to debate the exact dating and place of these works in Donatello's career. But they will no longer be able to ignore the technical evidence that has been revealed by this exemplary restoration. Donatello must have worked on a full scaffolding to carry out the stuccoes, just as the restorers did. Some of the tondi may, as Pietro Ruschi suggests, have been prepared beforehand during construction to receive the stuccoes: this would support an early date for the pendentive and lunette reliefs. The over-door figures must certainly have been carried out after the door surrounds themselves were inserted, as Ruschi also points out, and were therefore the latest element, apart from the bronze doors, to be executed. Characteristically, there are unfinished areas in the upper surfaces of the door-pediments – visible only from above. Finally, the cleaning of the over-door reliefs has made it clear that a different artist worked on the figures of Sts Cosmas and Damian, as Cristina Danti explains.

In making available a record of this restoration to a wider, English-speaking audience, the Magazine hopes both to increase informed awareness of the importance of conservation, and to make better-known some hitherto inaccessible masterpieces. We are very grateful to Cristina Danti and Maurizio Seracini for their enthusiastic and dedicated co-operation, and to Marilyn Perry of the Kress Foundation for her generous help with the costs of publication.

[1]P. RUSCHI: 'La Sagrestia Vecchia di San Lorenzo: per un disegno delle vicende costruttive', *Donatello e la Sagrestia Vecchia di San Lorenzo*, pp.15-23. A full bibliography of the extensive literature on the problem can be found on pp.112-15 of the Italian catalogue, which also publishes new documents from the S. Lorenzo archives.
[2]A. MANETTI: *Vita di Filippo Brunelleschi*, ed. G. Tanturli and D. De Robertis, Florence [1976], pp.109-10.

1. *St John on Patmos*, by Donatello.
Painted stucco. After cleaning.
Diameter c215 cm.

2. *St John Evangelist*, by Donatello.
Painted stucco. After cleaning.
Diameter c215 cm.

3. *'Martyrdom' of St John*, by Donatello.
Painted stucco. After cleaning.
Diameter c215 cm.

4. *Sts Stephen and Lawrence*, by Donatello. Painted stucco. After cleaning. 215 by 180 cm.

5. *Sts Cosmas and Damian*, by collaborator of Donatello. Painted stucco. After cleaning. 215 by 180 cm.

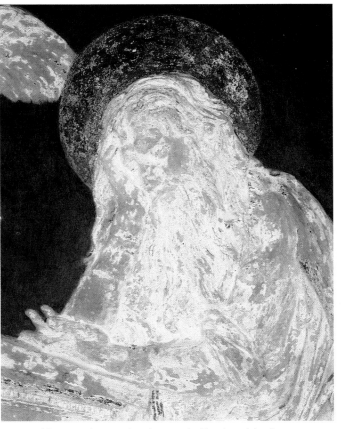

6a. Detail from *St John Evangelist*, photographed by ultra-violet fluorescence. After cleaning.

6b. Detail from *St John Evangelist*, in raking light. After cleaning.

6c. *St John Evangelist*. During cleaning.

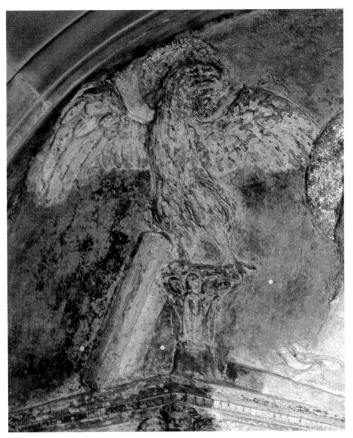

7a. Detail from *St John Evangelist*. During cleaning.

7b. Detail from *St John Evangelist*. After cleaning, in raking light.

7c. Detail from *St John Evangelist*. After cleaning, in raking light.

8a. Detail from *St John on Patmos*. After cleaning, in raking light.

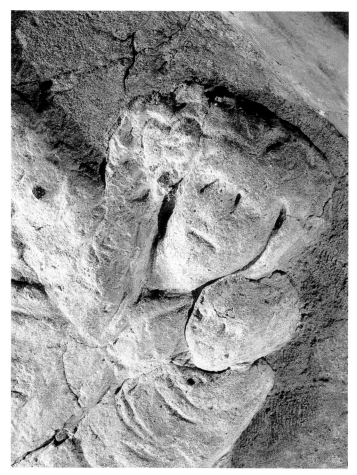

8b. Detail from *St John on Patmos*. After cleaning, in raking light.

8c. Detail from *St John on Patmos*. After cleaning, in raking light.

9a. Detail from *'Martyrdom' of St John*. After cleaning, in raking light.

9b. Detail from *'Martyrdom' of St John*. After cleaning, in raking light.

9c. Detail from *'Martyrdom' of St John*. After cleaning, in raking light.

10a. Detail from *St Stephen*. Before cleaning.

10b. Detail from *St Damian*. Before cleaning.

10c. Detail from *St Stephen*. After cleaning.

10d. Detail from *St Damian*. After cleaning.

From
Vertical
File

11a.

11b.

11c.

11d.

11a-f. Stages in the cleaning of *St Stephen*.

11e.

11f.

21

12a. *The Bull*. Detail from the altar chapel cupola. Fresco. Before cleaning.

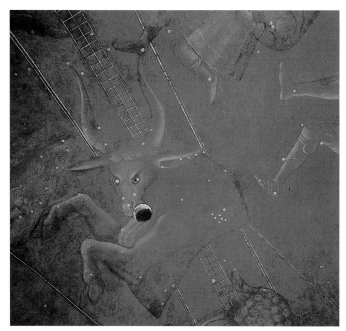

12b. *The Bull*. Detail from the altar chapel cupola. Fresco. After cleaning.

12c. *The Virgin*. Detail from the altar chapel cupola. Fresco. Before cleaning.

12d. *The Virgin*. Detail from the altar chapel cupola. Fresco. After cleaning.

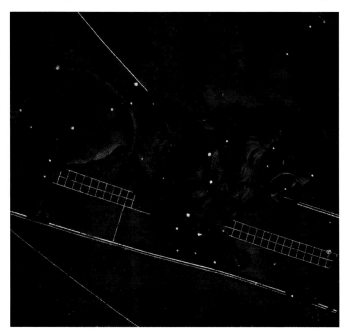

12e. *The Lion*. Detail from the altar chapel cupola. Fresco. Before cleaning.

12f. *The Lion*. Detail from the altar chapel cupola. Fresco. After cleaning.

Donatello's stuccoes restored: scientific examination and art-historical hypotheses

CRISTINA DANTI

Introduction

After an interval of about seventy years the Opificio delle Pietre Dure has returned to the task of restoring Donatello's stuccoes of the Old Sacristy of S. Lorenzo. It was indeed the Opificio which carried out a pioneering restoration of the reliefs between December 1912 and September 1913, cleaning off the white over-paint and carrying out what was described as 'appropriate' restoration. Then, as now, the Opificio was entrusted with its task by the Ministry via the Soprintendenza per i Beni Ambientali e Architettonici (then called the Soprintendenza ai Monumenti).

The 1912-13 restoration was of particular importance in the history of this sculptural ensemble and its conservation.[1] On all eight tondi Donatello's coloured surface was freed from the uniform layer of white which had covered it for at least two centuries (Alinari and Brogi photographs of c.1890 show the eight reliefs in their completely white state). We know very little about the fate of the reliefs in the three hundred years after their execution, but drastic operations of scraping off and replacing the white plaster reinforced with glue are recorded in an account book of 1756 in the S. Lorenzo archives.[2] The reliefs over the doors were not whitewashed on this occasion, but only dusted and cleaned.

The tondi in the pendentives and lunettes have, in fact, suffered a very different fate from the pairs of saints over the doors.[3] Despite originally performing a similar decorative function, they were differentiated early on: the reliefs in the tondi were treated as architectural plaster-work, to be regularly whitewashed, while the tabernacle reliefs were associated with the bronze doors below, and treated as though they, too, were of bronze: in fact an ochre tinting, in addition to the dirt, was found on their surface during cleaning.

The polychrome stuccoes of the Sacristy seem never to have

4. Detail from *St John Evangelist*. After cleaning, in raking light.

5. Detail from *St John on Patmos*. After cleaning, in raking light.

been liked, right from the start. As we know, they annoyed the Sacristy's architect, Brunelleschi; and even Donatello's collaborators and pupils may not have liked them, since they attempted nothing similar; Donatello himself may have been discontented with them, if it is correct – as suggested below – that he left them unfinished, and returned to give them a slightly different appearance.

The 1913 intervention by the Opificio marked the first bold appreciation of Donatello's '*colore*'. The present cam-

paign has gone even further, and the sensation aroused by the first cleaning tests has been fully justified in the finished results. Our work may arouse varying critical reactions; perhaps the stuccoes as they are today will not find favour, just as they failed to five centuries ago. But we are at least certain that we have enabled scholars and the public to experience something real and authentic, while preserving as conservators the greatest respect for the objects, on which we have worked to the best of our technical, scientific and historical abilities.

[1]The records are in the Archivio of the Opificio delle Pietre Dure, for 1912 and 1913, and in the Archives of the Basilica of S. Lorenzo, Insert 289, pos.A, No.36. After unsuccessful experiments with unspecified solvents, which were seen to be attacking the original colour, it was decided to clean '*a secco*', presumably with scrapers and small hammers as was then usual. The decisions about repainting and retouching were taken after a plenary meeting on 20th July 1913 of representatives of all the Conservation bodies together with Corrado Ricci, General Director for Antichità and Belle Arti for the Ministry of Education, and Luigi Cavenaghi, member of the Consiglio Superiore di Belle Arti. A special watch committee was appointed to oversee the observance of the criteria decided upon for this most delicate last stage of the restoration; and it was decided to carry out minimal re-painting only where absolutely necessary, for lack of knowledge of the original technique, and to avoid jarring effects. Precise instructions were given for the re-touchings to each medallion, and these were faithfully carried out. There is no written record, however, of the abundant use of drying oil as a fixative, in accordance with an old-established and almost universal practice.

[2]Archivio di S. Lorenzo, 10th September and 18th September 1756, Filza di ricevute, conti, note di spesa etc., del Capitolo di S. Lorenzo (1755-59); ins.69, a.f. 1756, ins.65, a.f. 1756; 12th June 1756, Filza di Ricevute etc. (1755-56), ins.117, a.f. 1756.

[3]The conservation history of the five stuccoes we have restored must certainly have been in line with their varying rates of deterioration. The roundels in the pendentives must always have been subject to infiltrations of water, and were therefore the most damaged and the most restored. Examples of conspicuous restoration include the upper part of St John's throne in the central tondo (see Fig.4); in other cases lack of comprehension led to failure to restore: e.g. the handle of the Apocalyptic Christ's scythe in the left tondo, which dropped off and was not replaced (Fig.5). The consistent whitewashing with 'bianco colato' on 'colla tedesca' may well have been aimed at conservation as well as aesthetic effect; the same may be said of the repeated heavy application of drying oils on each of the five reliefs, both in the tondi and over the doors. A precise 'reading' of all these interventions has been possible by comparing the data provided by chemical layer analysis with those produced by fluorescent ultra-violet photography.

Techniques and materials

The five reliefs of the altar wall may be divided into two groups: on the one hand the tondi in the pendentives; on the other the lunette tondo and the two reliefs above the bronze doors. The two groups are distinguished by differences in the composition of the materials, in their execution, and in the degree of relief of the modelling.

The pendentive tondi (Figs.5-11)
The pendentive tondi undoubtedly posed more difficulties of execution for Donatello, because of their location and the concavity of the surfaces to be filled. The problem here was like that of decorating a vault, entailing extra care in the construction of the oculus and in filling it with its decorative elements. This probably explains the need for the extensive array of nails driven into the masonry where elements in relief, however low, were to be attached. The heads of some of the nails can, for various reasons, be seen protruding from the surface (Figs.5, 6, 7); either because the plaster modelling has fallen off or been abraded; or because the final relief was lower than originally intended (see the upper part of the

6. Detail from *St John on Patmos*. After cleaning, in raking light.

7. Detail from *St John on Patmos*. After cleaning, in raking light.

rocks in *St John on Patmos*; or because the nails were used as decoration (like the bosses on the cauldrons in the '*Martyrdom*' *of St John*, formed from large round nail-heads; Fig.8), in general, however, the nails are completely engulfed in the substance of the relief, detectable only by infra-red thermovision at a depth of between two and ten millimetres from the surface (Figs.33-38).

The use of thickly clustered nails as a preparation and support for reliefs on a vault – often found later on, both in treatises and in actual practice – takes us directly back to the passages in Vitruvius about the preparation of stuccoed ceilings. The preparation he describes entailed using wooden lattice-work or reeds (*harundines graecae*) fixed to the masonry with metal nails, sometimes with large heads (*clavia muscaria*) to ensure a better hold.[1] These are probably the iron projections (by this time lacking the structure of wood or reeds) that Vasari cites as still visible in ancient buildings, and recommends as a means of keeping stucco 'suspended in the air', and of supporting any decorative projection.[2] And indeed the technique of anchoring projecting stucco on walls and vaults from the sixteenth century on follows the precepts laid down by Vasari.[3] In Brunelleschi's oculi, which are slightly concave, Donatello certainly had no need of lattice-work; for this gentle concavity provides – although this seems largely to have escaped the attention of scholars – one of the sources of expression for his complex and difficult perspective. The nails were used not only as a support but also to show where the relief was to go, as Vasari tells us: 'When the craftsman wants to execute a work in low relief, he first of all embeds the wall with nails, driving them in further or less, according to how the figures are to go.'[4]

After the preparation of the wall came the application of the material to make up the relief itself. Here there are at least three discernible stages, corresponding to different areas of the design; the background, the 'scenery' (the analogy with theatre design is not inapposite), and the figures and other prominently projecting elements. The first two (background and 'scenery') are of a uniformly reddish-pink material; this is effectively a '*malta*' or mortar, made of lime and sand, with the addition of ground-up brick. The use of what may loosely be called '*cocciopesto*' (literally 'pounded potsherds') brings us back once more to techniques known and recorded in Roman antiquity, '*Cocciopesto*' is cited by Vitruvius, Pliny the Elder, Palladius, Faventinus and Columella.[5] During the renaissance this practical technique could still be observed in the surviving Roman monuments. The Roman writers cite '*cocciopesto*' as an additive in the rough plaster, below fine *intonaco* (the smooth final plaster layer).[6] As a facing material it is mentioned in the context of pavements and baths or water tanks.[7] Archaeological sites confirm both these uses.

As far as we can discover, however, Donatello's extraordinary '*cocciopesto*', has no precise ancient or more recent analogue.[8] It is extraordinary in various ways. First its consistency is extremely fine, whereas all ancient '*cocciopesto*' is so coarse that the brick granules or pieces are easily visible. Second – and more important – this brick mixture is the surface, not the preparatory layer; and this at a time when the colour of bare brick – except of course in architectural contexts – was deemed unacceptable on its own, and was always

8. Detail from '*Martyrdom*' of St John. After cleaning, in raking light.

covered with other colours in order to simulate 'nobler' materials.[9]

Another peculiar characteristic is the colouristic function of this red plaster in Donatello's pictorial reliefs, both in its own right, and, as we shall see, as a ground for other pigments applied in fresco. Donatello's familiarity with terracotta has been stressed by scholars in discussions of his earlier career.[10] But here the material is undoubtedly used in a different manner and with different intentions; it embodies a most unusual and original unity of form and matter, of image and substance. With this red stucco Donatello composes mountains marked by decisive strokes of the spatula and clear stylus lines (*St John on Patmos*; Fig.9);[11] or he constructs perfect architectural settings in perspective with arches, piers, and staircases with steps and balustrades ('*Martyrdom*' of St John; Fig.10; col.pls.9b, 9c); these compose the theatrical scenery against which he places his figures and the objects which carry meaning.

For the figures Donatello used a white plaster composed only of lime and sand, i.e. a simple intonaco. They are thus detached from the background and from their field of action, standing out vividly even when modelled in the lowest relief. The narrative unfolds, lively and exuberant despite its enforced immobility. This exuberance, which exceeds the accepted norms of the period, has been noted by various critics, most recently by Timothy Verdon in connection with the S. Lorenzo pulpits,[12] and is visible in many of Donatello's reliefs: the example closest to ours (at least in a literal sense) is in the bronze doors of the Sacristy, where the figures lean against the frames of the compartments and partially overlap

9. Detail from *St John on Patmos*. After cleaning, in raking light.

10. Detail from *'Martyrdom' of St John*. After cleaning, in raking light.

11. Detail from *St John on Patmos*. After cleaning, in raking light.

them.[13] In the pendentive reliefs a further effect may be noted: the whole composition seems to 'hang' on the background of the Brunelleschian frame (and in fact the relief projects out of the frame in the lower part and noticeably recedes higher up). In this way not only is the overhanging position of the relief in some sense corrected, but the tondo almost seems to become an oval.

The parts in white stucco, like the red stucco background, are rapidly worked. Donatello certainly modelled and attached them with his hands, and finished them with very simple tools. In certain areas (the little trees on Patmos, the angel in the 'Martyrdom'; Fig.11; col.pl.9a) one can still see the clear imprint of his fingers, shaping and fashioning.

After these three stages of the work in plaster, Donatello then made a few, very significant, interventions in frescoed colour. On areas to be left in red stucco, he indicated shadow with a darker-toned red relief; and in certain areas of both narrative reliefs he used polychrome to create important expressive and perspectival effects; for example, in the foliage of the trees in the *St John on Patmos*, and in the bronze cauldron and flaming brands of the '*Martyrdom*' *of St John*. All the figures, however, are left absolutely white. The last intervention, made *a secco* (i.e. when the plaster was dry), was the coat of azurite blue in the skies, which also passes over the white stucco clouds; these shine through the transparent layer of paint as a shaded pale blue, apparently streaked by the wind.[14]

The seated St John and the two over-door reliefs

In the tondo showing the seated *St John Evangelist* (col.pl.2), and in the over-doors with the deacon and doctor saints (*Sts Stephen and Lawrence, Cosmas and Damian*, col.pls.4, 5), the relief is applied against the background of a flat wall surface. Thus the execution must have been quite straightforward, allowing the artist to use a fairly high degree of relief without encountering serious problems. Scientific tests showed a much less extensive employment of nails here (Figs.35, 37, 38),[15] and it is possible that a more substantial framework of wood, reeds or tow was used,[16] embedded in the wall,[17] and not detectable by the usual means of examination. Alternatively, it may be the case that the metal clusters are too deep to be reached by infra-red rays or by magnetometric surveys.

Only two layers of stucco are visible; background and figures. Both layers are composed exclusively of lime and clear sand, with no additives. All the figures are seen in perspectival foreshortening, and in the case of the Evangelist relief, the throne and desk also 'move' perspectivally, suggesting a viewing point slightly lower than the horizontal, but not as far down as the level of the pavement. The execution of the modelling varies noticeably from area to area: the faces and main areas of drapery are smoother; while the hair and beard of the Evangelist, and the fringes and finer clothing under the heavy draperies are flowing and strongly incised (Figs.12, 13); the eagle's feathers are treated with short strokes of the stylus – making the bird seem to vibrate on the point of flight

12. Detail from *St John Evangelist*. After cleaning, in raking light.

13. Detail from *St John Evangelist*. After cleaning, in raking light.

14. Detail from *St John Evangelist*. After cleaning, in raking light.

15. Detail from *'Martyrdom' of St John*. After cleaning, in raking light.

(Fig.14). Here too the tools used are undoubtedly of the simplest: hands first and foremost, then spatulae, pointed sticks, metal styluses.[18] The only note of frescoed colour is the red which gives a mulberry tone to the *a secco* azurite in the backgrounds of the figures, and makes a coloured foil to the foliage decoration around the frames, also in white plaster (col.pls.4, 5).

The white and gold layer

Up to now I have deliberately avoided discussing the final layer, the 'skin' over the white stucco in each relief. Here the restoration and scientific examination have produced some-what problematic results, for which only hypothetical explanations can at this stage be offered.

The first chemical analyses and the first cleaning tests already revealed the presence of a consistent overpainting with lead white in an oil medium over a gesso preparation, extended over all the figures and all the objects in white plaster on all five reliefs. This layer of white appears to be more substantial on the figure of the seated *Evangelist*, and still more so on the four saints of the overdoors. There subsequently came to light, below the dirt and the white lead repaints, an abundant and elaborate decoration in gold – especially rich on the garments of the saints, on the throne of the seated St John, and on the frames and foliage borders of the over-door reliefs.[19] In addition, a second coat of white and a second decoration in gold, with different motifs from the first, was found on the two saints (Stephen and Lawrence) of the left over-door. In the analysis of the different layers, no interruption of continuity was found between this skin and the other layers, even with the plaster itself.[20] Various intriguing hypotheses can be put forward as to when and by whom these pictorial interventions were made, and whether they were part of Donatello's original scheme, I do not, how-ever, believe that a definitive solution of these questions is yet possible.[21]

[1]M. VITRUVIUS POLLIO: *De Architectura*, ed. & tr. F. Granger, London [1956], pp.88 and 96 (Books VII, 3, and I-2-11).

[2]G. VASARI: *Le opere*, ed. G. MILANESI, Florence [1906], Vol.I, p.166.

[3]Thickly clustered nails, in this case joining the layers of stucco to the wooden support, are also present in the *Madonna dei Cordai*, attributed to Donatello (Museo Bardini, Florence). Here too, as I have had the opportunity to observe during the restoration of this relief, the nails function both as a support and as an indication of the greater or lesser projection of the parts in relief.

[4]VASARI, *op.cit.*, at note 2 above, p.166.

[5]VITRUVIUS, *ed.cit.*, at note 1 above, Bk.VII, 1, 3; VII, 4, 1; VIII, 7; PLINY THE ELDER: *Historia Naturalis*, Bks. 35, 46 and 36, 187; PALLADIUS, *De Re Rustica*, BK. IX, 9; FAVENTINUS: *De diversis fabricis architectonicis*, Bk. 6; COLUMELLA: *De re rustica*, Bk, I, VI, 13. These references were kindly supplied by ELIZABETH JANE SHEPHERD; see her essay 'L'antico e donatello, Archaeologia e sperimentazione tecnica', in *Donatello e la Sagrestia Vecchia*, pp.52-63. Vitruvius and Pliny the Elder were certainly known in the first half of the fifteenth century, and other references, however distorted and adapted, must have been transmitted through the 'recipe books' and the word-of-mouth workshop tradition – even more so than by the fifteenth- and sixteenth-century treatises known to us today.

[6]VITRUVIUS, *ed.cit.*, at note 1 above, p.98, Bk.VII, 4, 1. VASARI, when talking of Roman stuccoes, describes a preparation based on '*mattoni cotti*' or tufo (a soft and easily worked stone) which could be given the basic form of a cornice or figure, to which the various layers of modelled plaster were then applied (*ed.cit.*, at note 2 above, I, p.165). Vasari also mentions '*cocciopesto*' as a component of the inner layer of plaster in the preparation of a wall to be painted in oil (*ibid.*,

p.188), Alberti had already in the mid-fifteenth century cited '*cocciopesto*' as an ingredient in the first layers of *intonaco* in the antique manner, i.e. coarsely broken up into pieces 'as large as acorns, or fingers, or in some cases a whole hand' (L.B. ALBERTI: *De Re Aedificatoria*, Bk.VI, 9; the 1782 edition of Bartoli's translation was consulted). In the *Madonna dei Cordai*, too, '*cocciopesto*' was found in the first of the four layers of stucco, that closest to the support.

[7]VITRUVIUS, *ed.cit.*, at note 1 above, VII, 1 and VIII, 7; PLINY THE ELDER, Bk.36, 187; PALLADIUS, IX, 9; COLUMELLA, I, VI, 3; FAVENTINUS, 6 (see editions cited at note 5 above). All insist on the robustness and impermeability of the material when regularly coated with a layer of oil (*cf.* CENNINO CENNINI: *Il libro dell'arte*, ed. Neri Pozza, Vicenza [1971], pp.192-93, ch.CLXXV, and ALBERTI, *ed.cit.*, at note 6 above, p.150, Bk.VI, 10.

[8]The only comparable example seems to be the *Madonna and Saints* group by Niccolò di Luca Spinelli on the side door of the Duomo at Arezzo, datable in the 1390s, which is described by Vasari as in terra-cotta (VASARI, *ed.cit.*, at note 2 above, pp.192-93), but is actually in '*cocciopesto*' and probably executed *in situ*.

[9]See G. GENTILINI: 'Nella rinascita delle antichità', *La civiltà del cotto*, Florence [1980], p.71.

[10]See the valuable recent studies by: L. BELLOSI: 'Ipotesi sull'origine delle terre-cotte quattrocentesche', in *Jacopo della Quercia fra Gotico e Rinascimento*. Atti del Convegno di Studi, Siena, 1975, Florence [1977], pp.30-36; L. MARTINI: 'La rinascita della terracotta', in *Lorenzo Ghiberti – Materia e Ragionamenti*, Florence [1979], pp.208-24; and GENTILINI, *loc.cit.*, at note 9 above, pp.67-99. The Joshua in '*terra cotta*' or '*di mattoni e di stucco*' (Vasari) made by Donatello and Brunelleschi is the most relevant example cited by these authors for our purposes.

[11]It has not been possible to identify exactly what tools Donatello used. Apart from the trowel used to lay on plaster, we can guess that he used a few other tools to dig out, incise, smooth out and fill in the stucco. VASARI (*ed.cit.*, at note 2 above, I, pp.152-53), discussing models for sculpture in clay, wax or stucco, cites the use of bone, wooden or iron rods, flattened and/or toothed in the first two cases, and with double points in the last (*cf.* C. PICCOLPASSO: *Li tre libri dell'arte del vasaio*, ed. G. Conti, Florence [1976], pp.75-78, I, 13-14). Iron styluses had been used since antiquity for incising fresh intonaco; a more or less fine stylus with rounded point, similar to those used for drawing on tablets or parchment (CENNINI, *op.cit.*, at note 7 above, pp.10-13, 30. chs.VIII, X, XI, XXX). In antiquity VARRO (*De re rustica*, III, 17) and PLINY THE ELDER (*ed.cit.*, at note 5 above, XXV, 61, 149) mention the mural painter's use of the '*cestrum*', a metal tool with one spatulate end for smoothing and one sharpened end for incising (A. BARBEL and C. ALLAG: 'Techniques de preparation des parois dans la peinture murale romains', *Mélanges de l'Ecole Français de Rome*, 84, 2 [1972], p.984.

[12]T. VERDON: 'Stage space and projected space in the S. Lorenzo pulpits', paper given at the 74th Annual Meeting of the College Art Association of America, New York, 13th-15th February 1986.

[13]This was noted in a conversation on site between Timothy Verdon, Pietro Ruschi and the present author.

[14]The original azurite – a particularly delicate colour applied *a secco* – has almost completely disappeared and has been replaced by later repaintings. But examination under the microscope and chemical layer analysis has revealed traces of it, both on the red stucco ground and on the white stucco clouds.

[15]Thermographic tests in this case produced no result, either because the nail-heads were too small to give a thermal response, or because oily substances have impeded infra-red emission. By using a magnetic field, however, it was possible to identify the nails immediately below the surface, but not those more deeply embedded in the stucco.

[16]See VASARI on Roman stuccoes, *loc.cit.*, at note 2 above.

[17]In addition to the sources cited above at note 6, see ALBERTI, *ed.cit.*, at note 6 above, p.65, Bk.III, 11.

[18]It must be emphasised that nowhere in the five reliefs was any trace found of the use of stamps or moulds, or of pre-fabricated parts. ALBERTI, *ibid.*, Bk.VI, 9, p.148, mentions the use of moulds for stucco figures, but does not make clear whether they are to be executed in the workshop or *in situ*. There is no use either in the Old Sacristy stuccoes of ingredients such as powdered marble or glue.

[19]The technique of applying the gold is '*a missione*', the gold being applied together with a leaf of tin which acts as a support. CENNINI describes such a technique for use on plaster in wall paintings (*ed.cit.*, at note 7 above, pp.104-07, chs.XCVII, XCVIII, XCIX). In our case much of the gold has by now disappeared, exposing the tin, which has oxidised and become dark in colour.

[20]No deposits of dirt were found between the various layers constituting the test sample. This means that the stuccoes must have been painted shortly after their execution, unless we suppose that the plaster was perfectly cleaned before the painting. On the other hand, a fine layer of dirt was noted between the first and second decoration of the left-hand saints; in this case there was certainly a later intervention, probably in the seventeenth century, also involving many of the gilt flowers on the frame. Why only the left-hand saints should have been treated in this way is unclear; the right-hand saints show only sporadic re-applications of lead-white and gold, to fill in some gaps in the original.

[21] At the same time as these interventions the red of the framing was 'heightened' by the application of minium, vermilion and red lake (here too there is no interruption of continuity with the frescoed ground), and a second layer of azurite may have been applied in the skies (where the original colour appears unusually often).

16. Detail from *St John on Patmos*. After cleaning, in raking light.

17. Detail from *St John on Patmos*. After cleaning, in raking light.

18. Detail from *St John on Patmos*. After cleaning, in raking light.

19. Detail from *St John on Patmos*. After cleaning, in raking light.

20. Detail from *St John on Patmos*. After cleaning, in raking light.

21. Detail from *St John on Patmos*. After cleaning, in raking light.

22. Detail from *St John on Patmos*. After cleaning, in raking light.

23. Detail from *'Martyrdom' of St John*. After cleaning, in raking light.

24. Detail from *'Martyrdom' of St John*. After cleaning, in raking light.

25. Detail from *'Martyrdom' of St John*. After cleaning, in raking light.

26. Detail from *'Martyrdom' of St John*. After cleaning, in raking light.

27. Detail from *'Martyrdom' of St John*. After cleaning, in raking light.

28. Detail from *'Martyrdom' of St John*. After cleaning, in raking light.

29. Detail from '*Martyrdom*' *of St John*. After cleaning, in raking light.

30. Detail from *'Martyrdom' of St John*. After cleaning, in raking light.

31. Detail from *'Martyrdom' of St John*. After cleaning, in raking light.

32. Detail from *'Martyrdom' of St John*. After cleaning, in raking light.

37

Thermographic and Magnetometric Studies

GIUSEPPE RUFFA AND MAURIZIO SERACINI

The thermographic and magnetometric analyses of the tondi and over-door reliefs in the Old Sacristy were carried out in order to identify and locate objects inside the modelled reliefs or under the plaster surfaces which form the background of each composition. The different phases of the thermographic tests took place before and after the restoration.

The findings can be summarised as follows:

– Identification and location of components and irregularities in the wall which are not perceptible to the eye.

– Identification of metallic components (anchoring nails in the moulding) in the tondi and in the two over-door reliefs.

The choice of the two methods, infra-red thermography and long-distance metal detection, was designed to obtain complementary data in an absolutely non-invasive manner, excluding any physical contact between the equipment and the surfaces examined. These studies in fact, because of the principles of physics on which they are based, permit the characteristic natural properties of materials to be observed from a distance.

The results were positive on all five of the works examined, in that it was possible, integrating the data gathered, to locate irregularities in the support and metallic anchoring components, that is the nails discovered through this investigation. Specifically, the findings obtained from each of the five works can be summarised as follows:

The 'Martyrdom' of St John (right-hand tondo)

A dense network of nails, mostly with large round heads (similar to those visible to the naked eye), placed to support and anchor the relief, was revealed thermographically as documented by the montage of the relative thermographic images (Fig.33). These are present beneath both the perspective architecture, and the figures. The placement of the nails does not appear haphazard: rather they are distributed in a pattern and closely aligned with the position of the various projections to be supported (Fig.34). No irregularity was revealed in the supporting wall, but thermography was successful in identifying some small areas of the relief which had become separated from the support, appearing as lighter grey tones than those surrounding them.

Saint John the Evangelist (central tondo)

Nails were identified, distributed over the two figures depicted, the eagle and the Saint John, as well as on the throne on which the latter is seated (Fig.35). The base of the lectern and the moulding placed at the bottom of composition do not appear to contain any nails, even when observed with the magmometer. This suggests the presence of a different support system for the moulding in order to give the area a more or less consistent projection. A similar hypothesis can be advanced for the areas corresponding to the left leg and knee of the Saint. However, given the extreme thickness of these areas the presence of nails cannot be ruled out altogether, especially if they were placed deeply in the composition. If this were the case, the nails would not show up on the magnometer used to pinpoint the location of the nails, which is a low-powered instrument with a narrow range of observation. The wall which constitutes the background of the work did not give any indication of irregularities or anomalies of any kind.

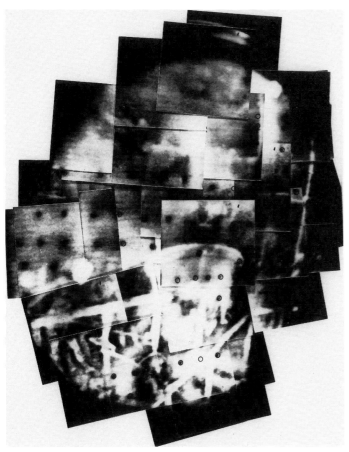

33. Montage of thermographic images of 'Martyrdom' of St John.

34. Placement of nails in 'Martyrdom' of St John.

35. Placement of nails in *St John Evangelist*.

36. Placement of nails in *St John on Patmos*.

Saint John on Patmos (left-hand tondo)

On the surface of this tondo protruding nails are clearly visible, especially on the trees and the dragon (Figs.5, 6). Others can be seen along the contours defining the mountain tops and in the figure at the top left. This tondo, like the '*Martyrdom*' of St John was the subject of thermographic tests carried out at two different times, before and after restoration. This was done both in order to be able to compare the results obtained under two different thermic conditions and to eliminate the possibilities of results owed exclusively to the presence of painted materials, which could produce adulterated thermic measurements relevant to the top layer of the surface.

During the first phase of the thermographic survey, carried out before restoration, the nail armature in this tondo was not visible. However, once the subsequent restoration removed the materials on the top layer which impede optimal thermographic results (fixatives, oil painting, protective layers) we were able to determine that the nail armature present in this composition continued to be noticeably less visible to infra-red than that in the right-hand tondo, and was often imperceptible.

The most likely explanation for this different thermic behaviour is that the nail heads are diverse in shape and size (mostly round with large heads in the right-hand tondo at right, and smaller with square heads in the left, with less surface available to IR). An oily substance is also present in the white lead, limiting the emission of IR by the materials below. For this reason, in the tondo depicting *St John on Patmos*, as well as in the over-door reliefs, we mainly used the magnetometric survey for the exact location of hidden metal components.

To be noted (Fig.36) is the rather regular distribution of the nails along three horizontal rows, placed so as to support the modelling which forms the hills in the backgrounds. Inside the figure on the top left the nailing is particularly dense and obviously distributed according to the weakest areas, such as the external contour and the major projections. In the thermographic study of the wall support an irregularity was revealed, made up of a clean, almost rectangular outline corresponding to the body of the dragon and bordered at the top by the stone frame. Given the quality of

the thermic findings obtained, one can hypothesise the presence of a lithic element probably emerging from the surrounding surface. A partial repair of the plaster can be discounted both because of the regularity of the outline of the anomaly revealed, and because of the quality of the thermic findings, so clearly differentiated from the findings obtained from the surrounding plaster.

Saints Stephen and Lawrence

The two figures, modelled on a vertical surface, are partially supported on a base constituted on the horizontal edge by the stone frame. Thus there seems to have been little danger of their detachment. The nail armature appears limited to the area below which the depth of the modelling is either minimal or shows sudden variations (Fig.37), such as in the gridiron, the projected folds in the drapery of the robes, in the hands, in other words wherever it would have been difficult to insert another type of support or material to anchor the moulding to the wall support. This has resulted in an irregularity in the area of Saint Lawrence's shoulder uncovered by the thermographic survey like those already discovered in the tondo depicting *St John on Patmos*. We found once again an area of clean, rectangular contours which seem to extend into the wall beneath the area occupied by the body of the figure.

The depth of the modelling does not allow a glimpse of the thermal emission which characterises the irregularity in question, but this shows up again between the left shoulder of St Lawrence and the stone frame, in almost exactly the same amount and at the same height as the other visible near the right shoulder of the saint. This suggests the continuity of a single element, probably of stone, sunk into the wall surface.

Saints Cosmas and Damian

Here the presence and distribution of the nail armature are similar to those found in the preceding relief. In this case there is a more regular distribution which follows the exterior outline of the figures, where modelling is lowest (Fig.38).

Given the abundance of folds, hollows, and protrusions in the drapery of the robes, the thermographic survey was once again accompanied by examination with a metal detector. In the central

37. Placement of nails in *Sts Stephen and Lawrence*.

38. Placement of nails in *Sts Cosmas and Damian*.

part of the figures (bust and legs) there was no sign of surface nailing. The greater depth of the modelling may have allowed the insertion of with different materials to support and anchor the stucco.

Photographic examination of colour-fluorescence by ultra-violet rays

CRISTINA DANTI AND MAURIZIO SERACINI

The examination of fluorescence by ultra-violet rays allows the state of conservation to be more objectively determined, giving a precise documentation of retouchings, restorations or overpainting present at the level of the pigment layer, or at the surface of the plaster.

For parts of the work not yet restored, ultra-violet fluorescence photography, besides helping the restorer in the task of removing dirt and extraneous materials, also allows the various interventions over time to be interpreted and located with precision. The repetition of such examination after restoration allows the present condition of the work, 'freed' of prior restorations, dirt, and alterations, to be verified and documented. Ultra-violet photography is particularly useful for wall paintings, in order to bring out the efflorescence of salts, organic and inorganic fixatives, repairs to the plaster, binders and consolidation treatment as well as abrasions or loss of the pigment or plaster.

The study of Donatello's stuccoes by ultra-violet light made it possible to identify interesting differences between the two pendentive stuccoes on the one hand and the central tondo and the two over-doors on the other. Three particularly significant examples demonstrate the use of this method as a supporting preliminary to restoration.

1. *The 'Martyrdom' of St John* was photographed in both UV fluorescence and natural light, in three different and successive phases: before, during and after restoration. The photograph in UV before restoration gives a general response of fluorescence ranging from golden yellow to dark brown: this intense fluorescence identifies the drying oil spread uniformly over the entire surface. Scattered but extensive areas which are minimally fluorescent (blue in the photograph) identify the efflorescence of sulphates and the protrusion of the raised plaster which has been partially pulverised.

The photograph in UV during restoration and, to be precise, after the elimination of surface oil, gives a more diversified response. There is an almost complete fluorescence of gold-yellow, more evident on the white plaster, indicative of the survival of more oily layers.

The fluorescence is now divided into distinctly different tones: light blue in the parts of the stucco which have been recently touched-up (such as the foot and the point of the pitchfork of the figure on the left and the point of the pitchfork of the figure on the right); grayish-blue where the saline efflorescence has 'peeled' the plaster.

The photographs in UV after restoration by contrast show an almost total elimination of yellow fluorescence (indicating the nearly complete removal of oils); a perfectly white response in the areas painted with white lead; a faint fluorescence (light blue or grayish-blue) in response to touched-up plaster or original plaster which had become uncovered; a non-fluorescence (dark blue in the photo) in areas showing strokes of azurite (even if old and no longer perceptible to the eye).

2. The *St John the Evangelist* relief (col.pls.6a-c, 7a-c) was photographed in UV fluorescence both during and after restoration. In the photo in UV taken during restoration, the area still to be cleaned is well-defined since it emits an intense golden-yellow fluorescence indicating the presence of a dense layer of oils. The wing of the eagle shows a gray-blue response above the yellow-gold which indicates a coating of whitewash. A more complicated picture is presented by the golden halo, in which different fluorescences appear, indicating a variety of conditions which in fact are evident in visible light. Considering the absolute non-fluorescence of pure metal, one can deduce that the areas of blue response are those in which gold applied in recent times is present. A more prominent fluorescence is caused by a painted gold, that is covered by oils or *missione* (oily varnish for attaching gold leaf), which could be present for various reasons, including further applications of metal. It should be pointed out here also that the background, which in visible light appears almost completely red *morellone*, in the photograph in UV fluorescence appears uniformly dark blue, having been covered at one time with an even coat of azurite, no longer visible today. In the photo in UV of the same detail (col.pl.6a), taken at the completion of restoration the overall yellow fluorescence has disappeared, owing to the complete elimination of oils. A light fluorescence survives however in the deeper crevices of the moulding, where the cleaning process could not completely remove the oil. The areas painted with white lead (which gives a white response) are quite different from the blank areas in which the surface of the plaster (which gives a bluish response) can be seen.

3. *The over-door reliefs* were photographed in UV fluorescence before, during and at the end of restoration.

The photograph in UV of Saint Damian before restoration highlights the uniform and thick layer of oils found on the surface (evidenced by the yellow-brown fluorescence).

In the photo in UV during restoration yellowish fluorescences could be noted in the areas painted with white lead, from the surfaces of which the layer of oils has not been completely removed. Even the gold leaf decorations appear fluorescent, since the gold had almost completely disappeared from the leaf, leaving however, at least in part, the oil varnish by which it had been attached. Here also could be noted the bluish fluorescence of the plaster, the surface of which emerges from gaps in the painting. The halo, which has also been cleaned of the thick, oily layers on the surface, presents (as in the tondo of the Evangelist) areas of blue response indicating a newer gold, or at least one that has not been covered by fixatives or oil varnishes.

An analogous result (that is a dark blue response) is obtained from the red *morellone* background, at one time covered entirely by azurite. It could be noted in the photo taken prior to restoration that this background gave off a light fluorescence, due also in this instance to the oil present on the surface.

The photo in UV at the end of restoration showed the completion of the cleaning operation with the consequent disappearance of the diffuse yellow fluorescence and the strong attenuation of the darker fluorescence concentrated in the depressions, in which the oil removal procedure: although carried out perfectly, was more difficult and perforce left incomplete.

Analytical, chemical and stratigraphic studies of painting layers and materials

MAURO MATTEINI AND ARCANGELO MOLES*

Premise

Before beginning restoration and the delicate phase of cleaning the stuccoes, which, on a first cursory examination, revealed a complex picture of several successive painting interventions, it was necessary to proceed with a careful chemical and stratigraphic investigation to evaluate precisely the nature and relationship of the painting materials present. For this purpose we carried out an extensive sampling, both in the form of fragments for the stratigraphic study and in the form of powder samples lifted selectively from the surface for the chemical analyses. The analytical technology used was infra-red spectrophotometry and chemical microanalysis.

The analyses of the cross sections proved to be extremely useful. Particularly interesting were the optical observations made by normal light and ultra-violet fluorescence and the colorimetric analysis, enabling identification and location of several of the more significant and recurring materials: especially gypsum, white lead, and proteinaceous and oily substances.

Chemical and stratigraphic analyses of the painting techniques and materials

a. Composition of the modelling stucco

The chemical and infra-red spetrophotometric analyses of the stucco used for the modelling showed in every case a simple and solely mineral composition, essentially based on lime and inert minerals.

It is therefore a normal plaster mortar, without any binders of an organic nature which would have resulted in a stucco of measurably less durability. The binding material, lime (calcium hydroxide), through the well-known spontaneous process of carbonation $(Ca(OH)_2 + CO_2 \rightarrow CaCO_3 + H_2O)$ determine the setting of the impasto with the formation of calcium carbonate (calcite).

On the other hand a more careful selection was made for the inert materials. Given that the results discussed here relate to samples gathered from the immediate surface of the relief, we were able to determine at these levels the use of two different types of impasto, one of which (white stucco) is used primarily for the figures and has an inert filler made up for the most part of colourless quartz and silicates. The other (red stucco), which appears in the backgrounds and in the architecture of the lateral tondos above, has an addition of powdered brick to give colour.

b. Painting technique of the blue backgrounds

The blue backgrounds against which the figures are placed in relief appear to be constructed with a different technique from that used on the figures. While in the drapery, the flesh, and the gilding a gypsum-based preparation is evident (below the first layer of painting) made up of proteinaceous and oily substances, which combine to create a painting techique analogous to that used on movable supports (wood and canvas), in the backgrounds the first layer of painting appears to be applied on the stucco-plaster according to traditional fresco procedure. In other words, the pigment is fixed directly by the lime of the plaster and an underlayer of preparation does not exist.

The analysis revealed the blue used in the background to be almost always azurite, except in one case in which indigo was identified below a layer of azurite. It is well known, however, that azurite, a pigment widely used in wall painting, does not tolerate a direct application on fresco, but must be dispersed in an organic binder.

In the stuccoes of S. Lorenzo the stratigraphic and chemical analyses clearly reveal the classic technique for blue backgrounds in wall painting: an application *a fresco* of so-called *morellone*, a mixture of red mineral ochre and carbon black; a successive painting with azurite dispersed in an organic binder. Since it was applied dry (probably with tempera), the layer of azurite has withstood the passage of time and events badly, and thus in many areas has fallen away, leaving areas bare with only the *morellone* preparation, or has been overpainted with azurite and other pigments, including many types of artificial ultramarine.

c. Painting technique of the robes and flesh

Above the stucco several layers are present which, because of their location and composition, were probably applied preparatory to painting. First there is a thin film of about 10-15μ, almost exclusively composed of proteinaceous materials. The colorimetric analyses suggest an animal glue, or, alternatively, a casein glue. Over this are two or three layers, with no solution of continuity and varying notably in thickness, in which the inert filler is composed of gypsum (calcium sulphate dihydrate) in a fine granulation, with a secondary presence of rougher and more transparent crystals. The binder is a proteinaceous and oily mixture which varies in composition from the innermost to the outermost layer, the proteinaceous component diminishing while the oily component increases.

All these layers must be considered a painting preparation on a base of gypsum, glue (or casein) and oil, applied in two or three coats, so as to obtain a more hydrophilic material (richer in binding proteins) in contact with the mineral mortar of the stucco, and gradually of a more oily nature externally, to receive the application of oil painting.

In the predominantly white drapery, with or without gold decoration, the primary paint layer is white lead with an oily binder. Above this the gilding has been applied, as discussed below in the paragraph on gilding.

In several samples a second layer was found, of white lead, but mixed with a greater quantity of oil. In many cases it has been applied to the gilding, though in others directly to the primary painting. Between the two white layers there is a very thin film which is not always either visible or analysable. This forms an unmistakable information of continuity between the two painting layers and points to the second as a later intervention. In many cases we found on the surface area, a second coat of gilding carried out with a technique similar to that used on the first coat.

The painting of the flesh was produced in a manner very similar to the painting of the drapery. We found once again a sequence of preparatory layers superimposed over the stucco plaster with compositions and thicknesses essentially equal to those found in the drapery. The painting layers were for the most part composed of white lead in oil, except for a single case in which an underlayer of ochre appears on part of the fragment.

Above the primary painting of the flesh, too, the stratigraphic analyses reveal nearly without exception the presence of a thin and intermittent film of separation and a recent overpainting with white lead, rich with oil and containing reddish ochres and lakes.

Finally, above the over-door figures the stratigraphic sections show a top-most layer of a bronze-like colour. This brown layer is made up of little more than a thin film with a base of ochre and carbon black, which has been applied on all the robes and flesh during a more recent restoration with the apparent intent to render their appearance more uniform.

d. Painting technique of the gilding

Comparing the various samples from areas in which gilding was used for haloes or decoration of the drapery, it was possible to identify several repeated sequences in the various samples which reveal the base technique of the gilding.

In all the samples examined the gilding followed an elaborate procedure, common in the wall paintings of this period. Instead of a simple gold leaf, a multilayered metallic laminate was built up. On a thin sheet of tin a thinner gold leaf was laid with oleoresin adhesive. The resulting laminate was most likely prepared separately (as in fact reported by Cennini) and then applied to the paint surface by means of an oil adhesive. The median thicknesses of the resulting structure areas follows:

oil adhesive for the tin	40-50 μ
sheet of tin	10-15 μ
oil adhesive for the gold	10-15 μ
gold leaf	2-3 μ

Under ultra-violet radiation the individual layers are well-defined in the cross sections. In particular the two oily layers present an intense fluorescence. However, the colour of the fluorescence is different from that of a simple drying oil owing to another component, probably a resinous substance, in the adhesive used to attach the gold which appears as a slightly more orange tone.

The layers below this gilding differ according to their context. Where the gilding is used to decorate the draperies or other figurative element, painting layers are found below. Thus for example, in the typical case of the decorated robes, a painting layer with a base of white lead lies under the gilding. In the haloes, on the other hand, where the gilding represents the only chromatic element, this lies directly on the whole of the preparatory layers of gesso and oily or proteinaceous binders, previously described.

In some cases the gilding is immediately followed by a second application of gilding obtained with an almost identical technique (e.g. the halo of Saint Lawrence). In other cases (several decorations of the robes for instance) the second gilding is separated from the first by a painting with white lead. The majority of samples however show only a single gilding.

e. Observations on the painting techniques of other areas.

Only a limited number of samples were taken from paint areas other than those composing the drapery, gilding, and background surfaces. Consequently it is not possible to define extensively the pictorial structure of these.

Nonetheless we can report several observations relative to the frames around the tondi and over-doors, and to the perspectival architecture of the tondi. The frame of the St Lawrence was particularly studied. Above the stucco is a chromatic layer of red brown applied a fresco, with a base of ochre, very similar to the layer of morellone noted in the blue backgrounds. Then we find the same ground with a base of gypsum, proteinaceous and oily substances which was found in the figures, robes, flesh, and haloes.

The painted layer visible in the sections was produced with vermilion and minium, used either separately or mixed, and finally covered with a thick but transparent coat rich with an oily binder, mixed with red lake and vermilion.

A different situation is observable in the few samples collected corresponding to the architectural motifs of the scene of the 'Martyrdom' of St John. On the plaster coloured with crushed brick a coat of red-brown ochre was applied a fresco. There follows an overpainting with a base of white lead mixed with red lake.

Conclusion

The analytical results and the stratigraphic studies discussed above, while making it possible to identify and locate the most recent repainting and touching-up, could not confirm the origin of that multilayered gypsum-based ground found above the stucco plaster or of the polychrome layer above.

*We should like to thank the personnel of the scientific laboratory who collaborated on the analyses and documentation, in particular C. Lalli, A. Aldrovandi, M.R. Nepoti, and N. Todorow.

The restoration

FABRIZIO BANDINI AND GUIDO BOTTICELLI

The state of conservation before cleaning

Before restoration great alteration was evident in the chromatic values of the pendentive tondi, owing to extensive darker and lighter patches visible on the surface. The light patches were caused by alterations in the oil applied during the last restoration of 1913. The poor state of the tondi was primarily due to infiltrations of humidity in the masonry structure of the pendentives. The consequent evaporation of pollutant materials on the surface resulted in an extensive crystallisation of salts such as nitrates and sulphates. The works as a whole were scarcely legible and it was impossible to decipher the technique of execution.

The central tondo (*Seated St John Evangelist*) was much more legible, although its relief appeared flattened because of the quantity of oil used as a fixative and the dust and smoke which had accumulated in the crevices of the modelling. Part of the sky and throne had been repaired, and in general the throne was much more damaged than the rest of the work, having suffered from the infiltrations of humidity that were also evident in the wall surface and pietra serena cornice.

The over-door stuccoes, as well as being very dirty, had been mistaken for terracottas because of their overall dark-brown surface, due to layers of overpaint in oil. The framing surrounds, although more legible, were in much the same state of conservation.

The restoration

The first stage was to remove all the loose dirt with a soft dry paint brush. Then a first cleaning of the surface was carried out with a small sponge dipped in de-ionised water to remove the impacted dust. After a certain number of cleaning tests aimed at the removal of the oil used in the earlier restoration and the small number of repaints (also in oil) it was decided to use a pack of ammonium carbonate. A sheet of Japanese paper soaked in de-ionised water was applied, to adhere as much as possible to all the projections of the relief. A film of micronised silica in a saturated solution of ammonium carbonate was then brushed on (col. pl.11b). A light but uniform pack was thus obtained over the whole surface, made up of successive portions of a median dimension of 10 by 15 sq. cm. The most suitable length of time for contact between the pack and the surface of the relief was judged to be thirty seconds, but could be as long as sixty seconds if the oily film to be removed was particularly thick. The reason for this choice of very brief applications was that, if the reagent had penetrated too far, it would have affected the binding oil of the zones painted in white lead. The pack was then removed (col.pl.11c) and the surface carefully washed with cotton wool pads soaked in de-ionised water, avoiding damage to the painted surface below. In some cases carbon dioxide was added to the water, to neutralise with its slight acidity the action of any ammonium carbonate left on the relief.

This stage allowed us to reach a uniform, homogeneous level of cleaning over the works as a whole, but was not in itself sufficient. The oil had in some areas penetrated the porous stucco, through gaps in the layer of lead white. So, in order to arrive at a greater equilibrium between the various parts, we completed the cleaning with a paint brush and a solution of ammonium carbonate, applied through a sheet of Japanese paper. The oil, made soluble by the ammonia, was then directly absorbed by the paper and completely removed (col.pls.11d-f).

The gold leaf was fixed before cleaning with a 3% solution of 'paraloid B 72' applied with a paint brush. However, much of the gilding was missing, revealing only the tin ground, blackened by oxidisation. The white lead areas were also fragmentary, as a large part of the colour had been removed during the earlier restoration along with the layers of whitewash. Furthermore, some fragments of paint had became detached, making it necessary to consolidate, using 5% acrylic resin in a watery emulsion. Given the extensive sulphate salts on the tondi, it would have been appropriate to treat them with barium hydroxide, but the oil-paint on the figures did not allow its use except in the left-hand tondo, where fewer figures appear; treatment was confined to the background surface. The consolidation of layers of plaster detached one from another was obtained by injecting acrylic resin thickened with calcium carbonate; but this was limited to very few and small areas.

On the left-hand over-door stucco we found a later layer of white lead and gilding which completely covered the earlier layer. The retention of this old restoration was justifiable from two points of view: first on conservation grounds because its removal would have compromised the original surface; second for historical reasons, because it had by now become part of the aesthetic character of the work. The right-hand over-door was more difficult to clean because of small abrasions and dirt impacted with the added oil of the bronze 'patina'. Here we used oxygenated water, exploiting its effervescent action. The blue background was also covered with oil and numerous repaints, which were removed.

Restoration of the paint

Here the aim was simply to restore equilibrium to the whole by a chromatic lowering of the missing areas which disturbed an overall 'reading'. The left-hand tondo, the most damaged, required 'chromatic selection' on the old and new repairs, to unify them with the surrounding stucco. The loss of the blue paint in the sky meant that the spatial planes could no longer be distinguished and the trees and clouds merged with the background. Hence it was decided to paint a light coat of azurite over the latter.

In the central tondo the red background was restored with 'chromatic selection' on the right-hand side, where there was a pre-existing repair. Here too, the blue ground was reinforced with an even layer of blue which was then roughened to match the general level of abrasion. The right-hand tondo required a more complex restoration because of its greater polychromy. The reintegration was aimed at restoring the original depth, bringing out the chiaroscuro and the shadows of the architecture.

The restoration of the over-doors was limited to a light in-filling of paint lacunas, without restoring the original support for the paint. The intention was to bring back the the overall equilibrium and aid legibility. The presence of oxidised tin without gold leaf created too sharp a contrast with the white of the figures, and so it was decided to reconstruct some of the gilding. No extra addition of blue to the background was necessary, and here intervention was limited to balancing the areas where the red preparation was over-evident.

39. *St John on Patmos*. Before cleaning.

40. *'Martyrdom' of St John*. During cleaning.

Observations after the restoration

CRISTINA DANTI

Among the very varied points which arose in the course of restoration of the Donatello reliefs, the most important, in our view, concerned their materials and methods of execution.

Above all the corner tondi surprised us by their extreme singularity: executed *in situ* on the wall, they find no parallels either in Donatello's work or in the entire range of Italian sculpture of the period.[1]

Such a direct mode of working, using rapidly drying materials, was clearly very difficult; it required very speedy execution, and gave extremely free and at times strongly expressionistic results. It should be borne in mind that, to guide him when starting on the reliefs, Donatello could make use only of preparatory sketches;[2] there are in fact many incised lines in the zones beneath the figures and the architectural settings, but they are drawn directly on to the plaster, without the use of cartoons. These lines are in any case not always respected: the figures and the corresponding architecture are sometimes carried out independently of or only partially following the first idea (Figs.41, 42, 43). Donatello worked freely, modelling primarily with his hands, and using few, very simple tools for the finishing. But this freedom should not be confused with liberty from intellectual canons and schemes. Indeed it should not be forgotten that the use of certain materials in certain situations can bring with it attitudes and results quite different from those which would have been produced by a different set of material conditions. These reliefs have a complex perspectival system (Figs.44, 45) and a strong reference to the antique (cf. Fig.46). Even though the artist's use of antique models here – as indeed elsewhere – is sporadic, it is nonetheless concrete and actual, starting from the materials themselves. In fact we have here a freshly remembered record of Donatello's visits to Rome, where, in the ancient monuments stripped of their marble facing, he saw the red-brick masonry with fragments of marble and stucco decoration adhering to it. This idea, which has been applied by Cristina Acidini to some Renaissance monuments in terracotta,[3] can, it seems to me, be extended to Donatello's red stuccoes, and in part explains their singularity.

It is hard to identify – still less to quantify – what

41. Detail from '*Martyrdom*' of St John. After cleaning, in raking light.

42. Detail from '*Martyrdom*' of St John. After cleaning, in raking light.

43. Detail from '*Martyrdom*' *of St John*. After cleaning, in raking light.

It is vital to underline the experimental character of these reliefs, in both conception and execution, an experimentation both of ideas and materials.[8]

A second series of observations may be made about the two over-door reliefs. These are undoubtedly part of a single decorative campaign, both architectural and sculptural, involving the whole of the walls on either side of the altar-chapel, which may be attributed to Donatello in the years immediately before he left for Padua in 1443. And yet, in the course of restoration, a striking point emerged that has not been noted before: the two pairs of saints appear to have been modelled by different artists. The St Stephen and St Lawrence, undoubtedly superior in quality (col.pl.4), are demonstrably modelled by hands used to 'adding and taking away, as those who work in wax, stucco or terra cotta, and are called in our vocabulary "maestri di stucco"',[9] to use Alberti's classification. By contrast, the St Cosmas and St Damian (col.pl.5) seem to have been executed by someone who operated 'only by taking away, like those who sculpt, removing all that is superfluous in the material, and reveal in the marble a form or human figure which was potentially there, but previously hidden',[10] that is, by a sculptor rather than a modeller, in Alberti's definition.

Even without accepting the dogmatic definitions of Alberti's *De Statua*, we must conclude that the second artist was not Donatello. Since our discovery, which he discussed with us on site, Sir John Pope-Hennessy has attributed the Sts Cosmas and Damian relief to Michelozzo (in a lecture given in Florence in January 1986). The suggestion is plausible – given the observations that have emerged concerning the architectural layout of the whole altar-wall – but it needs to be tested out in greater detail. For the moment we shall confine ourselves to pointing out the differences in technique, and to suggesting that a sculptor more 'classical' than Donatello was involved, one more oriented towards the revival of the noble and decorous aspect of Roman antiquity.

The last series of observations concerns the 'white and gold' layer, discussed in the technical section earlier on. As we have observed, this decoration shows no evidence of discontinuity with the stucco. And yet something prevents us from considering it completely original: that is the undeniable fact that this painting, together with its preparation, tends to clog up, mask and often blur the delicacy of the modelling and the lively stylus incisions on the surface. This is hard to reconcile with an artist's logical working procedure. No scientific test can – at least for the moment – cast further light, and the way remains open to hypothesis alone. For myself, I am convinced after the experience of the restoration and discussion with colleagues and conservators, that Donatello initially left the stucco as it was, demonstrating his appreciation for the material he had modelled with such care. The new plaster stood out resplendent against the reds and blues of the background. But at a second moment, perhaps after a temporary absence, if not indeed after his return from Padua,[11] he must have seen the huge strides made by his colleague Luca della Robbia in coloured glazed terra-cotta; in contrast to Luca's reliefs, the Old Sacristy stuccoes must have seemed much less vivid. It was perhaps at this stage that Donatello returned to the reliefs, brightening them with lead white –

Donatello saw in Rome, and during his journey there and back. Certainly he did not confine his study to 'classical' Roman antiquity, but also admired late antique, Hellenistic and Etruscan works. No doubt he was interested in a diversity of types of object: pavements and water-tanks as well as statues, sarcophagi and triumphal arches. It has often been observed that he preferred the least 'classical' aspects of the antique. In the case of the Old Sacristy stuccoes it should be emphasised that the antique references are specific, pointed and occasional, not uniform. One example is the almost incongruous insertion of small profile heads into the lower part of the '*Martyrdom*' *of St John* (Figs.41, 47); similar insertions appear also in the bronze *Feast of Herod* panel in Siena,[4] and in the marble relief of the same subject in Lille;[5] in fact these are the works which seem closest – despite the difference in materials – to the pendentive tondi. Detailed analogies may also be found with the *Ascension and delivery of the keys* marble relief in London (Victoria and Albert Museum);[6] the same cloud-streaked skies, the same spindly trees with umbrella-like foliage (similar, it is true, to Ghiberti's trees, but carrying a greater naturalistic and perspectival weight).

For all these reasons, we are not inclined to depart from the traditional dating of these reliefs, established by Janson (1434-43).[7] What seems important to revise is not the dating, but the interpretation of the 'spirit' of the works as objects.

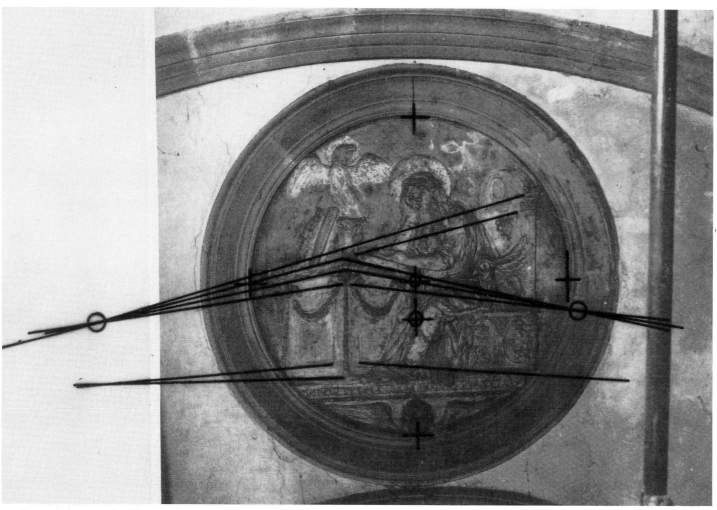

44. Perspectival system of *St John Evangelist*.

45. Perspectival system of *'Martyrdom' of St John*.

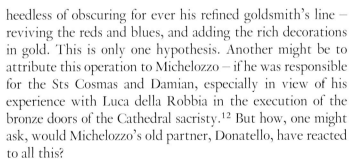

46. Antique relief in stucco with incised guide-lines. Stabian Baths, Pompei.

47. Detail from 'Martyrdom' of St John. Before cleaning.

heedless of obscuring for ever his refined goldsmith's line – reviving the reds and blues, and adding the rich decorations in gold. This is only one hypothesis. Another might be to attribute this operation to Michelozzo – if he was responsible for the Sts Cosmas and Damian, especially in view of his experience with Luca della Robbia in the execution of the bronze doors of the Cathedral sacristy.[12] But how, one might ask, would Michelozzo's old partner, Donatello, have reacted to all this?

A third hypothesis would be to suppose that both masters were employed simultaneously to paint the stuccoes, each on his own relief. That would explain the different (and superior) quality of the gold decoration which appears below the later repaints in the left-hand saints.

[1] With the exception of Niccolò di Luca Spinelli's 'cocciopesto' relief in Arezzo, mentioned above, p.19, note 8.

[2] The only reference to such drawings is completely apocryphal: Vasari's description in the *Ragionamenti* of Donatello showing Cosimo de'Medici his 'designs for the stucco decoration of the Old Sacristy', as depicted in the fresco of *Cosimo surrounded by artists* in the Palazzo Vecchio (VASARI, *ed.cit.*, at note 2 above, p.19, VIII, pp.98-99.

[3] C. ACIDINI: 'Il colore della città', in *La civiltà del cotto*, Florence [1980], pp.22-24.

[4] The relief dates to *c.*1425. See H.W. JANSON: *The sculpture of Donatello*, Princeton [1957], pp.65ff.

[5] Musée Wicar, Lille, datable *c.*1433-35 (*ibid.*, pp.129ff.) This work has striking analogies with the *'Martyrdom' of St John* relief; apart from the profile heads, the sequence of arches, the staircase with its handrail, and the legs of some figures in the background which appear suspended in the air.

[6] Datable *c.*1428-30; see JANSON, *op.cit.*, at note 4 above, pp.98ff.

[7] Janson dates the Old Sacristy reliefs to the years 1434-43 (*ibid.*, pp.132ff.), placing the over-door reliefs earlier than the tondi. Although agreeing with his general dating, we believe that the over-doors were done after the tondi, at the same period as the bronze doors below. Relevant to this conclusion are considerations about Donatello's intervention in the architecture of the altar wall, and the fact that his decorative programme was left incomplete (*cf.* P. RUSCHI's essay in *Donatello e la Sagrestia Vecchia*, pp.15-23.

[8] L. MARTINI: 'La rinascita della terracotta', in *Lorenzo Ghiberti – Materia e ragionamenti*, Florence [1978], p.208.

[9] L.B. ALBERTI: *De statua*, tr. C. Bartoli in *Della Architettura della Pittura e della Statua di Leonbattista Alberti*, Bologna [1782], p.323.

[10] *Ibid.*

[11] Detectable traces of deposited dirt between the intonaco and the pigment would have been formed after only a few years, especially in a closed environment such as the Sacristy.

[12] A.MARQUAND: *Luca della Robbia*, London [1914], pp.183 and 196.

[13] Considerations of this kind led to the decision taken during restoration to allow the first decoration to show through the second, even though it creates some visual and aesthetic confusion.

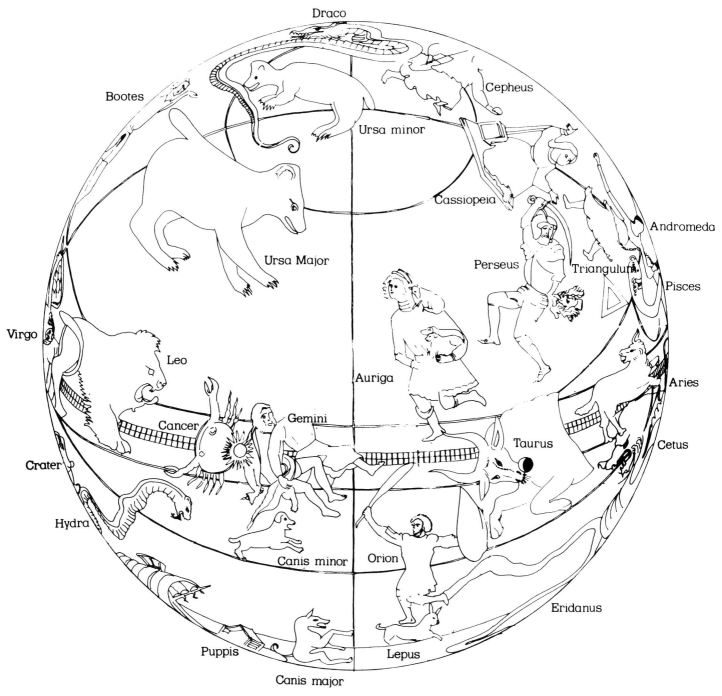

48. Diagram of the celestial hemisphere, showing outlines of the constellations (with names added); Altar chapel, Old Sacristy, S. Lorenzo, Florence.

The celestial hemisphere of the Old Sacristy and its restoration

ISABELLA LAPI BALLERINI

The small cupola over the altar chapel in the Old Sacristy of S. Lorenzo, decorated in the second quarter of the fifteenth century with a fresco of the northern celestial hemisphere (Fig.48; col.pls.12a-f) shown at a particular conjunction of constellations, is not mentioned in contemporary sources, and rarely appears in later guide books.[1] This is no doubt partly due to the difficulty of seeing the fresco from the ground, given that only one of the three windows of the altar chapel transmits light directly from the outside.[2]

The astronomical fresco was first studied in 1909 by Brockhaus,[3] who put forward the suggestion that the mathematician and astronomer Paolo dal Pozzo Toscanelli advised Cosimo de' Medici on the depiction of the stars; he attributed the painting to the elusive Giuliano d'Arrigo, known as Pesello. Brockhaus's shrewd observations (he also compared the fresco with the analogous vault in the Pazzi Chapel in S. Croce) must have escaped the notice of Aby Warburg, who was the first to attempt a complete astronomical reading of the vault.[4] Warburg claimed that the precise moment depicted corresponded to the position of the sun, moon and stars on 9th July 1422, given by an unconfirmed eighteenth-century source as the consecration date of the high altar of S. Lorenzo. Subsequently studied briefly by Saxl, Panofsky, Seznec and – more recently – by Dezzi Bardeschi and Battisti,[5] the painting was re-examined at close range by Parronchi, at the time of the restoration work on the roofs and internal vaults in 1977-78.[6] Assigning the idea for the fresco to Brunelleschi assisted by Paolo Toscanelli, Parronchi suggested that the moment depicted corresponded to the date of birth of Cosimo's eldest son Piero, born on 16th July 1416. Because of its mixture of late gothic and Masaccesque influences, Parronchi dated the execution of the fresco to c.1427 and, like Brockhaus, ascribed it to Giuliano Pesello, a painter whose name appears frequently in documents, but by whom no certain work survives.

In 1985 we decided to intervene quickly to restore the fresco, since its condition gave visible cause for concern.[7] The painting was practically illegible from the ground, obscured as it apparently was by dirt and smoke; moreover, extensive areas of efflorescent salts were visible, caused by repeated infiltrations of water, which had been stopped only recently. Once restoration was underway, we found that, in addition to the salts – alkaline sulphates, calcium oxalate, and, in smaller quantities, calcium nitrate – traceable with chemical tests,[8] there was a 'craquelure' over the whole surface, and the painting was obscured by at least four subsequent layers. First, on the outer surface, dust, atmospheric dirt and smoke; then extensive areas of repainting of the background with dark blue tempera which had become opaque and yellowed, and a repair to the intonaco in an area badly damaged by salts close to the base of the cupola; third was a thick filmy layer applied

with the thick streaky brushstrokes during an old 'restoration', which, because of a proteinous ingredient, had over time taken on a deep brown tone, dulling the brilliance of the colours below. Finally we found, adhering to the original paint, a last layer of repaints in strong tempera, less extensive, but tenacious and hard to remove; this had been used to fill in gaps in the background and to reinforce the profiles of many of the figures. Numerous restorations had profoundly altered the original values of the painting. Thus our intervention was not only one of conservation, but was aimed at an easier reading and more correct assessment of the original work.

In the analytical phase before the restoration itself, we were able to study the unusual technique of execution, which, for a mural painting, is extremely refined. After preparing a fairly thick intonaco and painting on to it a 'morellone' preparation (red ochre and lamp black), the artist painted entirely 'a secco' (i.e. on dry plaster), carrying out the background in a uniform blue pigment based on azurite, and then tracing the figures in brown ('vine black') and white highlights (white lead). He then picked out in gold the important astronomical details, i.e. the lines dividing the sky (meridians, ecliptic, equator, polar circles) and the numerous small stars. All these we found to be indicated with a fine metal-point incision and a white preparation. Since we found no trace of a preliminary drawing transferred by tracing or pouncing under the figures composing the constellations, we had to assume that the artist executed them freehand, with only the mapping of the astronomical preparation of stars and division lines to guide him.

To test out this disconcerting hypothesis, we had recourse to an infra-red reflectography camera,[9] which confirmed the absence of pouncing or cartoon. Instead it revealed under the finished figures a very clear and decisive linear underpainting in brown, corresponding perfectly to the final image. It must be said that in this very individual work drawing becomes painting, and vice-versa. Indeed the graphic character is one of the most unusual aspects of this fresco, and makes it quite untypical of contemporary mural painting; it is far closer to the trecento and quattrocento tradition of drawings made with a brush and white lead on dark-tinted paper. The infra-red examination confirmed the free-hand execution by revealing tiny but frequent corrections, as well as some larger pentimenti, observable in the front paws of the Bull, the head of the Serpent, and the tail of the Great Dog.

The cleaning was carried out in three stages: first the initial cleaning to remove the dirt and smoke and the background repaints susceptible to water; for this a cellulose pack soaked in de-ionised water was applied for c.4 hours over a sheet of Japanese paper. Next, to remove the efflorescent salts, a similar pack was applied repeatedly for periods of c.14 hours. For the final cleaning to remove the fixative and the more tenacious repaints, a very weak solution of Ammonium carbonate in water was applied with a paint brush over a layer of Japanese paper, removed after c.5 minutes.

Despite some lacunae and areas damaged by damp, the fresco emerged after cleaning in a far better state of preservation than we expected. Some corrections made by earlier restorers were visible under the heavy repaints, consisting of small anatomical changes, as in the ears and tail of the Hare. Reflectography carried out during cleaning confirmed the difference between the original pentimenti and these clumsy restorers' corrections.

An interesting art-historical point which emerged during the restoration was the presence of a second hand in the execution of the fresco. It had already seemed to us that the exquisite and 'mannered' handling of the Orion, the Great Dog, the Lion, and the Bull was incompatible with the earthy fleshiness of the Pollux, Bootes and Perseus figures. This was confirmed by the infra-red reflectography, which revealed a distinctly different painting technique. In itself this does not help much with the problem of attribution. The first hand is certainly that of the master, Pesello or whoever he may have been, while the second is probably that of a workshop assistant. In comparison with the International gothic virtuosity of the master, this second hand reveals an attempt at greater approximation to the 'real'; forms are shaped rather than traced, and the shadows are emphasised – a sign of the influence of Masaccio.

For the final phase of the restoration it was decided to integrate the missing areas of azurite, not using transparent layers of paint, which, against the red background, would have produced a dominant violet effect, but rather a denser colour based on azurite and applied 'selectively' (i.e. with a hatched technique). The aim of the retouching was to produce a harmonious overall effect, avoiding red patches of missing azurite, which would have disturbed a reading of the fresco as a whole. Finally the lost areas of gold on some of the stars and astronomical lines were restored: we considered this necessary for the recovery of the astrological meaning of the work, especially given its distance from the ground.[10]

[1]It is briefly mentioned by DOMENICO MORENI: *Delle tre suntuose Cappelle Medicee situate nell'Imp.Basilica di S.Lorenzo*, Florence [1813], p.269.

[2]Originally, before changes to the sacristy in the later fifteenth century, all three windows probably received direct light. See P. RUSCHI's contribution to the Italian catalogue, *Donatello e la Sagrestia Vecchia di S. Lorenzo*, pp.15-23.

[3]H. BROCKHAUS: *Michelangelo und die Medici Kapelle*, Leipzig [1909], pp.26ff.

[4]A. WARBURG: 'Die astronomische Himmeldarstellung im Gewolbe der alten Sakristei von S. Lorenzo in Florenz', *Mitteilungen des Kunsthistorischen Institutes in Florenz*, II [1912-17], pp.34ff. Gertrud Bing in an afterword to the reprinted version of Warburg's text, in *idem: Gesammelte Schriften*, I, Leipzig 1932, pp.366ff., comparing the vault with that of the Pazzi Chapel, proposed a date of 6th July 1439, the conclusion of the Council of Florence; this has been taken up by P. FORTINI BROWN: 'Laetantur Caeli: the Council of Florence and the Astronomical Fresco in the Old Sacristy', *Journal of the Warburg and Courtauld Institutes*, XLIV [1981], pp.176ff. For the present author's views, see note 10.

[5]For references, see E. BATTISTI: *Filippo Brunelleschi*, Milan [1976], pp.353ff.

[6]A. PARRONCHI: *Il cielo notturno della Sacrestia Vecchia di S. Lorenzo*, Florence, s.d. [1979], pp.3ff; see also *idem*, in *S. Lorenzo. La Basilica, la Sagrestia, le Cappelle*, ed. U. Baldini and B. Nardini, Florence [1984], pp.73ff. and in *Scritti di storia dell'arte in onore di Federico Zeri*, I, Milan [1984], pp.134ff.

[7]The restoration was undertaken in parallel with the work on the whole of the whole altar wall described elsewhere in this catalogue. The restoration work was carried out by the company De.Co.Art s.r.l. under the supervision of the present writer, with the assistance of geom. Raoul Paggetta.

[8]The chemical paint-layer analyses were carried out by Mauro Matteini and Arcangelo Moles of the Opificio delle Pietre Dure.

[9]The infra-red reflectography was carried out by E.di.Tech, s.r.l. under the direction of Maurizio Seracini.

[10]Further research on the painting of the cupola, including a new suggestion for the date represented in the fresco, was presented by the author in a contribution to the 'Giornate di studi su Donatello' at the Kunsthistorisches Institut in Florenz (18th-21st June 1986; in press). See also G. FORTI, I. LAPI BALLERINI, B. MONSIGNORI FOSSI, P. RANFAGNI: 'Un planetario del XV secolo', *L'astronomia*, ix, 62 [January 1987], pp.5ff.